J.O.Y.
Journal

Cathy Hanlin and Kayleigh Hanlin

BALBOA
PRESS

A DIVISION OF HAY HOUSE

To contact the authors, visit mindsempowered.com
or Facebook at Empowered Minds.
Interior Design by Pati Anderson and Victoria Hanlin
Cover art by Luciana Guerra

Balboa Press books may be ordered through booksellers or by contacting:

Balboa Press
A Division of Hay House
1663 Liberty Drive
Bloomington, IN 47403
www.balboapress.com
1 (877) 407-4847

Print information available on the last page.

ISBN: 978-1-9822-1093-9 (sc)
ISBN: 978-1-9822-1094-6 (e)

Library of Congress Control Number: 2018910149

Balboa Press rev. date: 09/14/2018

Thank you for purchasing *J.O.Y. Journal*! We know this journal will enlighten you on your journey of self-reflection and discovery.

Empowered Minds is committed to inspiring both kids and kids at heart to live a life full of self-acceptance, love, confidence, and joy. We are a mother-and-daughter team with a passion for helping others embrace what makes them unique and special. We are excited for you to join us on our journey and be a part of building a JOYful community.

We invite you to build a community of love and respect around you. We would love to have you join our tribe on Facebook and Instagram as well as on our website at www.mindsempowered.com.

As you travel through this journal creating collages and other creative pieces, if you would like to share your finished product with our community, find us on Facebook at Empowered Minds and post a photo of your work. Or you can like us on Instagram @JustOwnYou and tag us in your post.

This journal is dedicated to all women around the world—past, present, and future—who have discovered and owned their unique selves, shining as a bright guiding light for all of us to follow.

J.O.Y.

What Does It Mean to Just Own You?

All of us have unique qualities, values, and beliefs that help us decide what our life will be about. When we become aware of these gifts, we can easily find purpose in our lives. No two people have the same gifts or the same exact purpose in life.

Are you ready to have some fun discovering more about you? This journal is packed with fun activities to do and to think about. It has three objectives:

1. *Get to know more about yourself.* Really think about who you are on the inside and why.

2. *Get to know more about other people and who they are inside.* Explore the way you interact with others.

3. *Discover more about yourself in the world.* Dive deeper into how you choose to be unique and how you own the best parts of you.

Are you ready to **grow, give, love, and live**? Turn the page to start exploring the ideas and activities you can choose from.

Let's Get Started!

My Biography

Start by writing down some details and fun facts that make you uniquely you.

My full name:_____

My favorite nickname:_____

My birthday:_____

The town I live in:_____

Other people in my family:_____

_____

_____

_____

The name of my school and current grade level:

_____

My favorite thing to do with my friends:_____

My favorite thing to do by myself:_____

My favorite part of school:_____

I love learning about and exploring such topics as:

_____

_____

The funniest thing I have ever done:_____

My favorite color(s):_____

My favorite song(s):_____

My favorite singer(s) or band(s):_____

_____

My least-favorite singer(s) or band(s):_____

_____

My favorite food:_____

My least-favorite food:_____

The best book I ever read:_____

The worst book I ever read:_____

My favorite movie:_____

My least-favorite movie:_____

Other things I want people to know about me:_____

_____

_____

_____

_____

_____

_____

_____

_____

_____

Share your responses with Mom, Dad, a friend, or someone else you care about. Then ask them to share what they would put in their biography.

My Daily Review

Every day has a best part. Some days have a challenging part too. By reflecting on your day, you can build a habit that can help you create more good days. Here is how to do it:

1 Find a special stone the next time you are outside. Call this your *reflection stone*.

2 Hold your reflection stone in your hands, close your eyes, and sit silently.

3 While sitting in silence, ask and answer these questions:

- What was best about today?
- What was most challenging about today?
- How did I do at working through today's challenge?
- What did I learn?
- What am I most grateful/appreciative for today?

4 With your eyes still closed, say thank you for all that happened today.

5 On the next page or pages in the back of your journal, write down what you thought about during your daily reflection. Write five things you are grateful for today and why you appreciate each one.

Find a time every day to do this. It is best to pick the same time every day. It can be when you wake up, get home from school, finish dinner, or go to bed. Use the pages in the back of your journal to capture your thoughts.

My Daily Review

_____
_____
_____
_____
_____
_____
_____
_____
_____
_____
_____
_____
_____
_____
_____
_____

REFLECTION
_____
_____
_____
_____
_____

My Best Day Ever

Some days are so great that you just know you will remember them forever. One of your best days may have been when you had a blast with your very best friends, did something fun alone or with a family member, or even aced a test.

What were you doing on some of your best days?

Day 1:_____

Day 2:_____

Day 3:_____

Circle the day above that you would like to write more about. You have the following questions to guide you.

When was this day? (You can include details like how old you were, how long ago it was, what season it was, and what day of the week it happened on.)

_____

_____

_____

Who was with you, and what were they doing? If you were alone, how did it feel?

_____

_____

What did you see, hear, think, and feel that day?

_____

_____

_____

_____

_____

_____

_____

What do you always want to remember about that day?

_____

_____

_____

_____

_____

_____

_____

Beyond the book: ask others to tell you about their best day ever.

 # Crazy Cool

Singer and music producer Pharrell Williams says, "No human being is the same; we are like snowflakes. None of us are the same, but we are all *COOL*." The things that make you who you are, make you unique. These are the things that make you stand out from others in fantastic ways!

Think of all the things that make you cool. For example: *I am ... kind, considerate, courageous, mindful, honest, patient, observant, trusting, funny, helpful, knowledgeable, neat, healthy, and playful.* Write them down in the spaces below:

_____ _____ _____

_____ _____ _____

_____ _____ _____

On the next page, create a collage that shows all of the things that are unique, fantastic, and cool about you. Your collage can include anything that can be pasted to the next page. Here are some suggestions you can use to get started:

♥ Include words and pictures that you write, draw, print, or cut out of magazines.

♥ Print some of your own photos.

♥ Attach personal artifacts like a fortune from a fortune cookie, a handwritten note, or a movie-ticket stub. If the artifact is too large to paste onto the page, draw it or take a picture and print it.

Be super creative!

I Love These Cool Things about Myself

Admire your collage from "Crazy Cool". What things do you see that you really love about yourself? Did you get all the things that you love about yourself into your collage? If not, you can add more at any time.

In the boxes below, capture in words or pictures the top three things you really know and LOVE about yourself.

I am

I am

I am

Bookmark this page and read it out loud often.

My Future Self

Right now, you are perfect, and you are growing. People continuously change. We learn new skills, go to new places, meet new people, and try new things. We are always evolving.

Did you know that you can decide how you progress? Your dreams and plans for the future shape how you change, and you can choose to change in ways that make you happy. How about that for good news?

This one takes a little bit of visual thinking, and you can do it easily. Let's imagine you are now ten years in the future. Make another collage to show the new things that are going to be cool, unique, and fantastic about you in the future.

What are the new things you will love most about yourself in the future?

Next year	In five years	Ten years and after
_____	_____	_____
_____	_____	_____
_____	_____	_____
_____	_____	_____
_____	_____	_____
_____	_____	_____

Use your journal pages in the back if you need more room. On the next page, create a collage that shows the new things that will be unique and fantastic about you in the future. Your collage can include anything that can be pasted to the next page.

Remember, you can be super-creative!

Letter to Yourself

You can accomplish a lot in a year. We all wonder, *What will it be like in the future?* It's fun to think about the future, and your imagination can help. Imagine yourself one year from now.

Imagine what's going on in your life that makes you happy. What types of activities are you doing? What have you accomplished? What are you doing for fun? What makes you proud? Who are you surrounding yourself with: school friends, siblings, new community friends?

Use the lines on the next page to write your older self a letter. Congratulate your older self on all you have learned and accomplished. Remind your future self of important things you know about yourself today and memories that are important. Share with your future self the special hopes and dreams that you have for your life.

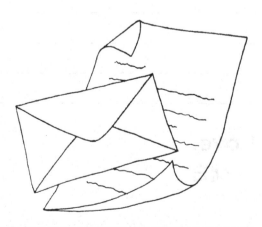

Dear future self,

_____

_____

_____

_____

_____

_____

_____

_____

_____

_____

_____

_____

_____

_____

_____

_____

Love,
ME

Quotes That Guide

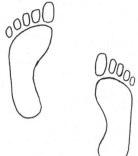

Quotes are everywhere: on T-shirts, notebooks, posters, websites, and even in this book. Why are quotes used so much? Quotes can touch our hearts, inspire us, and help us to understand and push past life's tough times. Quotes can also help us to remember happy experiences.

Let's explore quotes to help you find your favorite. Here are a few places to look:

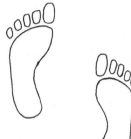

- the lyrics to your favorite songs
- a line from a favorite movie or book
- inspirational people like Eleanor Roosevelt, Emma Watson, Ruth Bader Ginsburg, Oprah, Millie Bobby Brown, or Gabby Douglas
- quotes about emotions that you enjoy feeling, such as love, kindness, joy, silliness, or gratitude
- the people you admire

Write down your favorite quote:

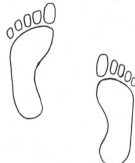

_____

Draw a picture, write a poem or short story, or create an abstract design that tells the meaning of your quote.

Favorite Quote

 # Tune In to You

Music is a part of life. It influences your mood. The type of music you enjoy is also a part of your style. What would your life be like without music?

_____

_____

_____

What are some of your favorite songs? Close your eyes and really listen to them. You can do this by imagining the songs or playing them out loud. How do they make you feel? What do they make you think about? Fill in your answers below.

Name of a favorite song:

_____

When I hear this song, I feel and think about:

_____

_____

_____

Now think about your unique song—a song you will write for yourself. You could share it with the whole world, or no one else ever has to hear this song. It is up to you. What is the style of music of your song?

_____

_____

_____

_____

What key words are in your song?

_____

_____

_____

_____

Would there be instruments or just vocals in your song?

_____

_____

_____

If there are instruments, which ones are in your song?

_____

_____

_____

_____

How do you feel about your song?

_____

_____

_____

_____

What colors and images come to mind when you hear your song?

_____

_____

_____

Why is this song important to you?

_____

_____

_____

_____

How will this song help you to be *YOU*?

_____

_____

_____

_____

_____

_____

On the next page, write the words to your song.

My Song

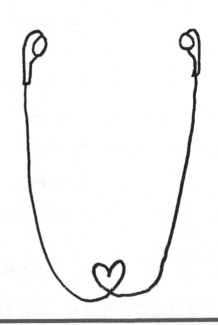

Magical Wish

If a genie popped out of a lamp and said she would give you three wishes, what would you wish for? Would you wish for material things for yourself, like a cool jacket? You could wish for something that your family would want, like a new bike for your little sister or concert tickets for your older brother. You could even use one of the wishes to help the global community, like wishing for a cure for cancer or a world without bullying.

If you were granted three wishes, what would they be?

1._____

2._____

3._____

Why would you choose these three wishes?

_____

_____

_____

_____

_____

Thank You

Many people move in and out of your life; some bring you joy, while others bring challenges. There are people in your life who push you to be better and others who support you.

Write a thank you note to three people who have most influenced your life. Use the following pages to brainstorm and write your letters. Here are a few examples to get you thinking:

Dear Aunt Daphne,

Thank you for being such a cool aunt! I am so glad I get to go on all kinds of fun adventures with you. William and I always have a blast with you. I also want to thank you for being there for me when I need you. I am really grateful that you are such a good listener, and when I have problems, you give me advice on doing the right thing. You are the best aunt ever!

Thank you,
Charlotte

Dear Mom and Dad,
Thank you for being such amazing parents. I know I sometimes have a hard time following your rules, or we fight and argue. But whenever I need you, you are supportive and kind. I am also thankful for all the things you give me, like birthday gifts and new school clothes. I love you both so much!
Love,
Me, your awesome kid

Dear little sister,
Thank you for being the best sister in the whole world! I know we may argue and fight sometimes, but I would never change one minute of the time we get to spend together. I will always be around when you need someone to play with or talk to. You're the greatest!
Love,
Your cool big sister

Write your letter here. Feel free to share it with the person you wrote to if you wish.

_____

_____

_____

_____

_____

_____

_____

_____

_____

_____

_____

_____

_____

_____

_____

_____

_____

_____

_____

_____

_____

Write your letter here. Feel free to share it with the person you wrote to if you wish.

_____

_____

_____

_____

_____

_____

_____

_____

_____

_____

_____

_____

_____

_____

_____

_____

_____

_____

_____

Write your letter here. Feel free to share it with the person you wrote to if you wish.

_____

_____

_____

_____

_____

_____

_____

_____

_____

_____

_____

_____

_____

_____

_____

_____

_____

_____

_____

_____

_____

Be a Detective

Ever wonder what it would be like to be someone else? Do you ever imagine living in a different time or in a different country? We all wonder what it would be like to walk in someone else's shoes.

Find someone who is older than you to interview. This person could be a parent, grandparent, older cousin, teacher, or mentor. Below are several possible questions; ask a few of them or all of them. You can also create your own questions.

I am interviewing _____

What year were you born? _____

Where did you grow up? _____

What was it like growing up there?_____

What did you want to be when you grew up? _____

Did you follow that path?_____

In your opinion, what is the most interesting historical event you've lived through?

_____

Tell me about that event. Where were you when it happened?_____

_____

How old were you? _____

How do you feel about it?_____

What is your favorite childhood memory?_____

Who is your favorite musician?_____

What is your favorite book and/or movie? Why?_____

Do you recommend I read it or see it? If so, at what age?_____

If there is one moment in your life that you could relive, what would it be? _____

_____

Is there a moment in your life you would change? Why?_____

What makes you unique? What do you love most about yourself?_____

What do you want to be remembered for?_____

In what way has your uniqueness helped you in your life?

_____

On the next page, write up your interview as if it were an interview
with a celebrity that will appear in a magazine.

My Interview with

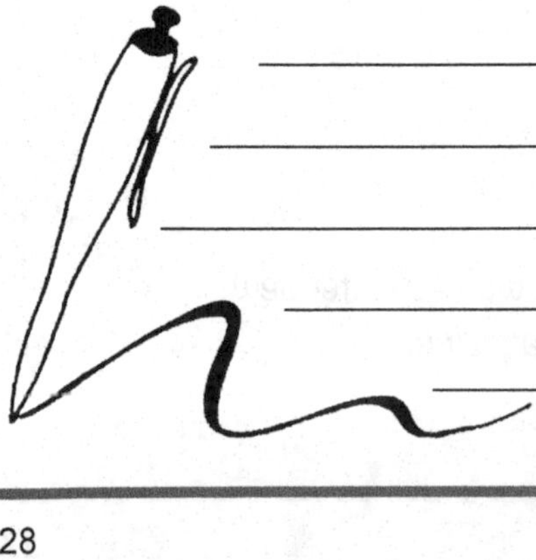

After the interview, think about what you learned about that person. Did anything they say surprise you? Would you like to live that life? Learning about the past can help us create a better future.

How can you incorporate this person's experiences and life lessons into your future?

_____

_____

_____

_____

_____

_____

_____

_____

_____

_____

_____

_____

_____

_____

_____

_____

_____

_____

_____

Beep, Beep!

Today, technology is all around us. From sleek cell phones to mini iPads, we can communicate with anyone and everyone with a push of a button. We can have hours of conversation with someone and never see them in person. We no longer need face-to-face discussions to get information; instead, we use emails, texting, photos and even emojis to communicate. What would happen if all that quick and easy communication went away? You are about to find out.

Take the pledge below not to use one of the tools of technology for a certain amount of time, such as two hours or a couple days. View all of the guidelines before making your pledge.

I pledge not to do one of the following for _____ hours/days:

→ go on Facebook, Twitter, Instagram, Snap Chat or another favorite social media
→ text or read texts
→ use any gaming app

Guidelines
1. Pick a time frame when you do not have to use technology for a school project or other needs.
2. Tell others in advance of your pledge so they are aware and can communicate with you through other channels.
3. Make sure the time frame is specific and realistic.

Reflection Questions

What was it like not having that communication tool?

_____

_____

How did it feel to go without it?

_____

_____

How did you choose to communicate without it?

_____

_____

What did you do with the time you gained by giving up technology?

_____

_____

What was it like when you reconnected to technology?

_____

_____

Would you do it again? Why or why not?

_____

_____

Is our world better or worse with mass technology within easy reach?

_____

_____

Exploring New Communities

Did you know that there are **195** different countries in the world? Did you know that there are more than **19,000** different cities just in the United States? That is a lot of new places to see!

It is always fun and exciting to explore and learn about new areas of the world. This can mean exploring the next town over from yours or discovering an entirely new country. Exploring new areas allows us to learn and understand how others experience life.

Although travel is amazing, sometimes we do not have enough time and money to go to all the new places we wish to see. Today we are lucky to have excellent technology to help us. With technology, we can see the great places we wish to visit from the comfort of our home or local library. Then we can plan future visits to some of these amazing new places.

Choose a city, state, or country you would like to visit. Research that area through travel blogs, search engines, social media, or visitor's bureau websites. Answer the questions below and use the following space to include magazine pictures or drawings of the place you wish to visit.

I want to visit:

_____

_____

What is the
history of the
city or country?
Was it filled with
peaceful times or
times of war?

_____

_____

_____

What would
you do or see
there? Why did
you choose this
location?

_____

_____

_____

_____

What
transportation
would you use to
get around?

_____

_____

_____

Would there be a
language barrier?
If so, how would
you overcome it?

_____

_____

_____

Making an Impact in the Community

Did you know young girls just like you are making a difference in their communities? These girls are impacting people all over the world. One place to discover women from the past and present who changed the world and helped to bring attention to important community issues is at the National Women's History Museum's website.

Books are another resource to find strong women changing the world. For example, *I Am Malala*, by Malala Yousafzai, is about this young girl's bravery in fighting for the right to education for girls in Pakistan.

What interests you? Is it music, theatre, art, exploration, science, education, a specific time in history, or perhaps something else? Write what interests you below.

_____

_____

Select an impactful woman or girl in one of your areas of interest. She can be from the past or present. Do research on your own on this particular person who is making an impact in the world. What did you learn from her story?

What did you learn about their stories?

_____

_____

What do you admire about this girl or woman?

_____

_____

What makes the individual you learned about unique?

_____

_____

Like the unique person you picked, you too can change the world around you—in small and big ways. What are some ideas you have for helping to make your community, family, school, country, or world a better place?

_____

_____

_____

_____

_____

_____

_____

_____

_____

_____

_____

_____

_____

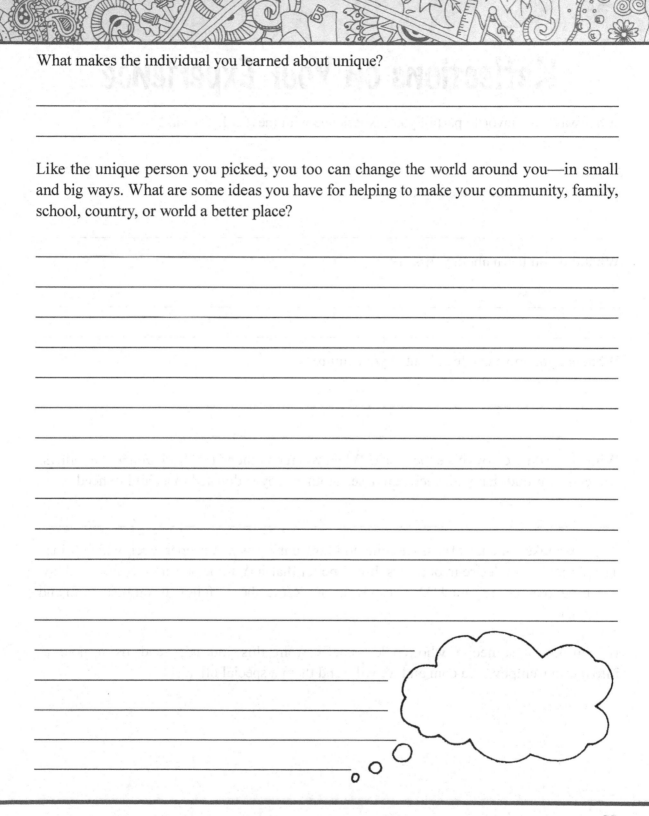

Reflections on Your Experience

What was your favorite part of your experience with the *J.O.Y. Journal*?

_____

Which activities did you enjoy the most?

_____

What did you learn about yourself?

_____

_____

What are you most excited about in your future?

_____

_____

Who else would enjoy this experience? When you recommend the *J.O.Y. Journal* to others, you can be proud that with each purchase, another copy is donated to a child in need.

_____

When we take time to reflect, we come to know ourselves at a deeper level, which brings a JOY that we all desire in our lives. It is time for that JOY to be present in your life daily. It is time to embrace your J.O.Y.: Just Own You! Remember to follow us on Instagram and Facebook.

If you know someone who could benefit from this journal, send us a note at info@mindsempowered.com and we will send them a special offer.

Fabulous Five

Date____/____/____

Today, I am most excited about-

☆ ☆ ☆ — ☆ ☆ ☆

Today I will...

_____
_____
_____
_____
_____
_____
_____
_____
_____
_____
_____
_____
_____

☆ ☆ ☆ — ☆ ☆ ☆

Thankful thoughts:

Learning lessons:

What was the best thing about today? What am I celebrating?

My Daily Review

_____
_____
_____
_____
_____
_____
_____
_____
_____
_____
_____
_____
_____
_____
_____
_____
_____
_____

REFLECTION
_____
_____
_____

Fabulous Five

Date___/___/___

Today, I am most excited about-

Thankful thoughts:

Learning lessons:

☆ ☆ ☆ — ☆ ☆ ☆

Today I will...

_____
_____
_____
_____
_____
_____
_____
_____
_____
_____
_____
_____
_____

☆ ☆ ☆ — ☆ ☆ ☆

What was the best thing about today? What am I celebrating?

My Daily Review

_____
_____
_____
_____
_____
_____
_____
_____
_____
_____
_____
_____
_____
_____
_____
_____

REFLECTION
_____
_____
_____

Fabulous Five

Date___/___/___

Today, I am most excited about-

★ ★ ★ — ★ ★ ★

Today I will...

_____

_____

_____

_____

_____

_____

_____

_____

_____

_____

_____

★ ★ ★ — ★ ★ ★

Thankful thoughts:

Learning lessons:

What was the best thing about today? What am I celebrating?

My Daily Review

_____

_____

_____

_____

_____

_____

_____

_____

_____

_____

_____

_____

_____

_____

_____

_____

_____

REFLECTION

_____

_____

_____

Fabulous Five

Date____/____/____

Today, I am most excited about-

Thankful thoughts:

Learning lessons:

★ ☆ ★ — ★ ☆ ★

Today I will...

_____

_____

_____

_____

_____

_____

_____

_____

_____

_____

_____

_____

★ ☆ ★ — ★ ☆ ★

What was the best thing about today? What am I celebrating?

My Daily Review

_____
_____
_____
_____
_____
_____
_____
_____
_____
_____
_____
_____
_____
_____
_____
_____

REFLECTION
_____
_____
_____

Fabulous Five

Date___/___/___

Today, I am most excited about-

Thankful thoughts:

Learning lessons:

Today I will...

_____
_____
_____
_____
_____
_____
_____
_____
_____
_____
_____

What was the best thing about today? What am I celebrating?

My Daily Review

_____
_____
_____
_____
_____
_____
_____
_____
_____
_____
_____
_____
_____
_____
_____
_____
_____

REFLECTION
_____
_____
_____
_____

Fabulous Five

Date____/____/____

Today, I am most excited about-

☆ ☆ ☆ — ☆ ☆ ☆

Today I will...

_____
_____
_____
_____
_____
_____
_____
_____
_____
_____
_____

☆ ☆ ☆ — ☆ ☆ ☆

Thankful thoughts:

Learning lessons:

What was the best thing about today? What am I celebrating?

My Daily Review

_____
_____
_____
_____
_____
_____
_____
_____
_____
_____
_____
_____
_____
_____
_____
_____

REFLECTION
_____
_____
_____
_____

Fabulous Five

Date____/____/____

Today, I am most excited about-

Thankful thoughts:

Learning lessons:

★ ☆ ★ — ★ ☆ ★

Today I will...

_____
_____
_____
_____
_____
_____
_____
_____
_____
_____
_____
_____

★ ☆ ★ — ★ ☆ ★

What was the best thing about today? What am I celebrating?

My Daily Review

REFLECTION

Fabulous Five

Date____/____/____

Today, I am most excited about-

☆ ☆ ☆ — ☆ ☆ ☆

Today I will...

_____
_____
_____
_____
_____
_____
_____
_____
_____
_____
_____
_____
_____

☆ ☆ ☆ — ☆ ☆ ☆

Thankful thoughts:

Learning lessons:

What was the best thing about today? What am I celebrating?

My Daily Review

_____
_____
_____
_____
_____
_____
_____
_____
_____
_____
_____
_____
_____
_____
_____
_____

REFLECTION
_____
_____
_____

Fabulous Five

Date____/____/____

Today, I am most excited about-

Thankful thoughts:

Learning lessons:

☆ ☆ ☆ — ☆ ☆ ☆

Today I will...

_____

_____

_____

_____

_____

_____

_____

_____

_____

_____

_____

☆ ☆ ☆ — ☆ ☆ ☆

What was the best thing about today? What am I celebrating?

My Daily Review

_____
_____
_____
_____
_____
_____
_____
_____
_____
_____
_____
_____
_____
_____
_____

REFLECTION
_____
_____
_____

Fabulous Five

Date___/___/___

Today, I am most excited about-

☆☆☆ — ☆☆☆

Today I will...

_____
_____
_____
_____
_____
_____
_____
_____
_____
_____
_____

☆☆☆ — ☆☆☆

Thankful thoughts:

Learning lessons:

What was the best thing about today? What am I celebrating?

My Daily Review

_____

_____

_____

_____

_____

_____

_____

_____

_____

_____

_____

_____

_____

_____

_____

_____

_____

REFLECTION _____

_____

_____

Fabulous Five

Date____/____/____

Today, I am most excited about-

★ ★ ★ — ★ ★ ★

Today I will...

_____
_____
_____
_____
_____
_____
_____
_____
_____
_____
_____
_____
_____

★ ★ ★ — ★ ★ ★

Thankful thoughts:

Learning lessons:

What was the best thing about today? What am I celebrating?

My Daily Review

_____
_____
_____
_____
_____
_____
_____
_____
_____
_____
_____
_____
_____
_____
_____
_____
_____
_____

REFLECTION

Fabulous Five

Date____/____/____

Today, I am most excited about-

★ ★ ★ — ★ ★ ★

Today I will...

_____
_____
_____
_____
_____
_____
_____
_____
_____
_____
_____

★ ★ ★ — ★ ★ ★

Thankful thoughts:

Learning lessons:

What was the best thing about today? What am I celebrating?

My Daily Review

REFLECTION

Fabulous Five

Today, I am most excited about-

★ ★ ★ — ★ ★ ★

Today I will...

_____

_____

_____

_____

_____

_____

_____

_____

_____

_____

_____

_____

Thankful thoughts:

Learning lessons:

★ ★ ★ — ★ ★ ★

What was the best thing about today? What am I celebrating?

My Daily Review

_____

_____

_____

_____

_____

_____

_____

_____

_____

_____

_____

_____

_____

_____

_____

_____

_____

REFLECTION

Fabulous Five

Date____/____/____

Today, I am most excited about-

Thankful thoughts:

Learning lessons:

☆ ☆ ☆ — ☆ ☆ ☆

Today I will...

_____
_____
_____
_____
_____
_____
_____
_____
_____
_____
_____

☆ ☆ ☆ — ☆ ☆ ☆

What was the best thing about today? What am I celebrating?

My Daily Review

_____

_____

_____

_____

_____

_____

_____

_____

_____

_____

_____

_____

_____

_____

_____

_____

REFLECTION

_____

_____

_____

Fabulous Five

Date____/____/____

Today, I am most excited about-

Thankful thoughts:

Learning lessons:

★ ☆ ★ — ★ ☆ ★

Today I will...

_____
_____
_____
_____
_____
_____
_____
_____
_____
_____
_____
_____
_____
_____

★ ☆ ★ — ★ ☆ ★

What was the best thing about today? What am I celebrating?

My Daily Review

_____
_____
_____
_____
_____
_____
_____
_____
_____
_____
_____
_____
_____
_____
_____
_____
_____
_____

REFLECTION
_____
_____
_____
_____

Fabulous Five

Date___/___/___

Today, I am most excited about-

Thankful thoughts:

Learning lessons:

☆ ☆ ☆ — ☆ ☆ ☆

Today I will...

_____
_____
_____
_____
_____
_____
_____
_____
_____
_____
_____
_____

☆ ☆ ☆ — ☆ ☆ ☆

What was the best thing about today? What am I celebrating?

My Daily Review

_____
_____
_____
_____
_____
_____
_____
_____
_____
_____
_____
_____
_____
_____
_____
_____
_____

REFLECTION

Fabulous Five

Date___/___/___

Today, I am most excited about-

☆☆☆ — ☆☆☆

Today I will...

_____

_____

_____

_____

_____

_____

_____

_____

_____

_____

Thankful thoughts:

Learning lessons:

☆☆☆ — ☆☆☆

What was the best thing about today? What am I celebrating?

My Daily Review

_____
_____
_____
_____
_____
_____
_____
_____
_____
_____
_____
_____
_____
_____
_____
_____

REFLECTION
_____
_____
_____

Fabulous Five

Date____/____/____

Today, I am most excited about-

☆ ☆ ☆ — ☆ ☆ ☆

Today I will...

_____

_____

_____

_____

_____

_____

_____

_____

_____

_____

☆ ☆ ☆ — ☆ ☆ ☆

Thankful thoughts:

Learning lessons:

What was the best thing about today? What am I celebrating?

My Daily Review

_____
_____
_____
_____
_____
_____
_____
_____
_____
_____
_____
_____
_____
_____
_____
_____

REFLECTION _____
_____
_____
_____

Fabulous Five

Date____/____/____

Today, I am most excited about-

☆ ☆ ☆ — ☆ ☆ ☆

Today I will...

_____

_____

_____

_____

_____

_____

_____

_____

_____

_____

Thankful thoughts:

Learning lessons:

☆ ☆ ☆ — ☆ ☆ ☆

What was the best thing about today? What am I celebrating?

My Daily Review

_____
_____
_____
_____
_____
_____
_____
_____
_____
_____
_____
_____
_____
_____
_____

REFLECTION
_____
_____
_____

Fabulous Five

Date____/____/____

Today, I am most excited about-

Thankful thoughts:

Learning lessons:

☆ ☆ ☆ — ☆ ☆ ☆

Today I will...

_____
_____
_____

_____

_____

_____

_____

_____

_____

_____

_____

☆ ☆ ☆ — ☆ ☆ ☆

What was the best thing about today? What am I celebrating?

My Daily Review

_____

_____

_____

_____

_____

_____

_____

_____

_____

_____

_____

_____

_____

_____

_____

REFLECTION _____

_____

_____

Fabulous Five

Date___/___/___

Today, I am most excited about-

Thankful thoughts:

Learning lessons:

☆ ☆ ☆ — ☆ ☆ ☆

Today I will...

_____
_____
_____
_____
_____
_____
_____
_____
_____
_____

☆ ☆ ☆ — ☆ ☆ ☆

What was the best thing about today? What am I celebrating?

My Daily Review

REFLECTION

Fabulous Five

Date___/___/___

Today, I am most excited about-

Thankful thoughts:

Learning lessons:

☆ ☆ ☆ — ☆ ☆ ☆

Today I will...

_____
_____
_____
_____
_____
_____
_____
_____
_____
_____
_____
_____
_____

☆ ☆ ☆ — ☆ ☆ ☆

What was the best thing about today? What am I celebrating?

My Daily Review

_____
_____
_____
_____
_____
_____
_____
_____
_____
_____
_____
_____
_____
_____

REFLECTION _____
_____
_____

Fabulous Five

Date____/____/____

Today, I am most excited about-

Thankful thoughts:

Learning lessons:

☆ ☆ ☆ — ☆ ☆ ☆

Today I will...

_____
_____
_____
_____
_____
_____
_____
_____
_____
_____

☆ ☆ ☆ — ☆ ☆ ☆

What was the best thing about today? What am I celebrating?

My Daily Review

_____

_____

_____

_____

_____

_____

_____

_____

_____

_____

_____

_____

_____

_____

_____

_____

REFLECTION _____

_____

_____

_____

Fabulous Five

Date____/____/____

Today, I am most excited about-

Thankful thoughts:

Learning lessons:

☆☆☆ — ☆☆☆

Today I will...

_____
_____
_____
_____
_____
_____
_____
_____
_____
_____
_____

☆☆☆ — ☆☆☆

What was the best thing about today? What am I celebrating?

My Daily Review

_____
_____
_____
_____
_____
_____
_____
_____
_____
_____
_____
_____
_____
_____
_____
_____
_____
_____

REFLECTION
_____
_____
_____

Fabulous Five

Date____/____/____

Today, I am most excited about-

Thankful thoughts:

Learning lessons:

☆ ☆ ☆ — ☆ ☆ ☆

Today I will...

_____
_____
_____
_____
_____
_____
_____
_____
_____
_____
_____

☆ ☆ ☆ — ☆ ☆ ☆

What was the best thing about today? What am I celebrating?

My Daily Review

_____
_____
_____
_____
_____
_____
_____
_____
_____
_____
_____
_____
_____
_____
_____
_____

REFLECTION
_____
_____
_____
_____

Fabulous Five

Date___/___/___

Today, I am most excited about-

☆☆☆ — ☆☆☆

Today I will...

_____
_____
_____
_____
_____
_____
_____
_____
_____
_____
_____

☆☆☆ — ☆☆☆

Thankful thoughts:

Learning lessons:

What was the best thing about today? What am I celebrating?

My Daily Review

_____
_____
_____
_____
_____
_____
_____
_____
_____
_____
_____
_____
_____
_____
_____
_____
_____
_____

REFLECTION
_____
_____
_____

Fabulous Five

Date____/____/____

Today, I am most excited about-

Thankful thoughts:

Learning lessons:

☆ ☆ ☆ — ☆ ☆ ☆

Today I will...

_____
_____
_____
_____
_____
_____
_____
_____
_____
_____
_____

☆ ☆ ☆ — ☆ ☆ ☆

What was the best thing about today? What am I celebrating?

My Daily Review

_____
_____
_____
_____
_____
_____
_____
_____
_____
_____
_____
_____
_____
_____
_____
_____
_____

REFLECTION
_____
_____
_____

Fabulous Five

Date___/___/___

Today, I am most excited about-

Thankful thoughts:

Learning lessons:

☆ ☆ ☆ — ☆ ☆ ☆

Today I will...

_____
_____
_____
_____
_____
_____
_____
_____
_____
_____
_____

☆ ☆ ☆ — ☆ ☆ ☆

What was the best thing about today? What am I celebrating?

My Daily Review

REFLECTION

Fabulous Five

Date___/___/___

Today, I am most excited about-

☆☆☆ — ☆☆☆

Today I will...

_____
_____
_____
_____
_____
_____
_____
_____
_____
_____
_____
_____

☆☆☆ — ☆☆☆

Thankful thoughts:

Learning lessons:

What was the best thing about today? What am I celebrating?

My Daily Review

_____
_____
_____
_____
_____
_____
_____
_____
_____
_____
_____
_____
_____
_____
_____
_____

REFLECTION
_____
_____
_____
_____

Fabulous Five

Date____/____/____

Today, I am most excited about-

★ ☆ ★ — ★ ☆ ★

Today I will...

_____

_____

_____

_____

_____

_____

_____

_____

_____

_____

_____

_____

★ ☆ ★ — ★ ☆ ★

Thankful thoughts:

Learning lessons:

What was the best thing about today? What am I celebrating?

My Daily Review

_____

_____

_____

_____

_____

_____

_____

_____

_____

_____

_____

_____

_____

_____

_____

_____

_____

REFLECTION

_____

_____

_____

_____

Fabulous Five

Date___/___/___

Today, I am most excited about-

Thankful thoughts:

Learning lessons:

☆☆☆ — ☆☆☆

Today I will...

_____
_____
_____
_____
_____
_____
_____
_____
_____
_____
_____
_____

☆☆☆ — ☆☆☆

What was the best thing about today? What am I celebrating?

My Daily Review

_____
_____
_____
_____
_____
_____
_____
_____
_____
_____
_____
_____
_____
_____
_____
_____

REFLECTION
_____
_____
_____

Fabulous Five

Date___/___/___

Today, I am most excited about-

Thankful thoughts:

Learning lessons:

★ ☆ ★ — ★ ☆ ★

Today I will...

_____
_____
_____
_____
_____
_____
_____
_____
_____
_____
_____
_____

★ ☆ ★ — ★ ☆ ★

What was the best thing about today? What am I celebrating?

My Daily Review

_____

_____

_____

_____

_____

_____

_____

_____

_____

_____

_____

_____

_____

_____

REFLECTION _____

_____

_____

Fabulous Five

Date____/____/____

Today, I am most excited about-

★ ☆ ★ — ★ ☆ ★

Today I will...

_____
_____
_____
_____
_____
_____
_____
_____
_____
_____
_____
_____
_____
_____

★ ☆ ★ — ★ ☆ ★

Thankful thoughts:

Learning lessons:

What was the best thing about today? What am I celebrating?

My Daily Review

REFLECTION

Fabulous Five

Date____/____/____

Today, I am most excited about-

★ ★ ★ — ★ ★ ★

Today I will...

_____
_____
_____
_____
_____
_____
_____
_____
_____
_____
_____
_____

★ ★ ★ — ★ ★ ★

Thankful thoughts:

Learning lessons:

What was the best thing about today? What am I celebrating?

My Daily Review

REFLECTION

Fabulous Five

Date___/___/___

Today, I am most excited about-

☆ ☆ ☆ — ☆ ☆ ☆

Today I will...

_____
_____
_____

_____
_____
_____
_____
_____
_____
_____
_____
_____

Thankful thoughts:

Learning lessons:

☆ ☆ ☆ — ☆ ☆ ☆

What was the best thing about today? What am I celebrating?

My Daily Review

_____
_____
_____
_____
_____
_____
_____
_____
_____
_____
_____
_____
_____
_____
_____
_____

REFLECTION
_____
_____
_____

Fabulous Five

Date____/____/____

Today, I am most excited about-

Thankful thoughts:

Learning lessons:

☆ ☆ ☆ — ☆ ☆ ☆

Today I will...

_____
_____
_____
_____
_____
_____
_____
_____
_____
_____
_____

☆ ☆ ☆ — ☆ ☆ ☆

What was the best thing about today? What am I celebrating?

My Daily Review

_____
_____
_____
_____
_____
_____
_____
_____
_____
_____
_____
_____
_____
_____
_____
_____
_____
_____

REFLECTION
_____
_____
_____

Fabulous Five

Date____/____/____

Today, I am most excited about-

Thankful thoughts:

Learning lessons:

☆☆☆ — ☆☆☆

Today I will...

_____
_____
_____
_____
_____
_____
_____
_____
_____
_____
_____

☆☆☆ — ☆☆☆

What was the best thing about today? What am I celebrating?

My Daily Review

_____

_____

_____

_____

_____

_____

_____

_____

_____

_____

_____

_____

_____

_____

_____

REFLECTION

_____

_____

_____

_____

Fabulous Five

Date____/____/____

Today, I am most excited about-

☆ ☆ ☆ — ☆ ☆ ☆

Today I will...

_____
_____
_____
_____
_____
_____
_____
_____
_____
_____
_____
_____

☆ ☆ ☆ — ☆ ☆ ☆

Thankful thoughts:

Learning lessons:

What was the best thing about today? What am I celebrating?

My Daily Review

_____
_____
_____
_____
_____
_____
_____
_____
_____
_____
_____
_____
_____
_____
_____
_____

REFLECTION
_____
_____
_____

Fabulous Five

Date____/____/____

Today, I am most excited about-

Thankful thoughts:

Learning lessons:

☆☆☆ — ☆☆☆

Today I will...

_____
_____
_____
_____
_____
_____
_____
_____
_____
_____
_____
_____
_____
_____

☆☆☆ — ☆☆☆

What was the best thing about today? What am I celebrating?

My Daily Review

_____
_____
_____
_____
_____
_____
_____
_____
_____
_____
_____
_____
_____
_____
_____
_____

REFLECTION
_____
_____
_____

Fabulous Five

Date____/____/____

Today, I am most excited about-

Thankful thoughts:

Learning lessons:

Today I will...

_____
_____
_____
_____
_____
_____
_____
_____
_____
_____
_____
_____

What was the best thing about today? What am I celebrating?

My Daily Review

REFLECTION

Fabulous Five

Date___/___/___

Today, I am most excited about-

☆ ☆ ☆ — ☆ ☆ ☆

Today I will...

_____

_____

_____

_____

_____

_____

_____

_____

_____

_____

_____

Thankful thoughts:

Learning lessons:

☆ ☆ ☆ — ☆ ☆ ☆

What was the best thing about today? What am I celebrating?

My Daily Review

_____
_____
_____
_____
_____
_____
_____
_____
_____
_____
_____
_____
_____
_____
_____
_____

REFLECTION
_____
_____
_____

Fabulous Five

Date___/___/___

Today, I am most excited about-

☆ ☆ ☆ — ☆ ☆ ☆

Today I will...

_____
_____
_____
_____
_____
_____
_____
_____
_____
_____
_____
_____
_____
_____

Thankful thoughts:

Learning lessons:

☆ ☆ ☆ — ☆ ☆ ☆

What was the best thing about today? What am I celebrating?

My Daily Review

REFLECTION

Fabulous Five

Date____/____/____

Today, I am most excited about-

☆ ☆ ☆ — ☆ ☆ ☆

Today I will...

_____
_____
_____
_____
_____
_____
_____
_____
_____
_____
_____
_____

☆ ☆ ☆ — ☆ ☆ ☆

Thankful thoughts:

Learning lessons:

What was the best thing about today? What am I celebrating?

My Daily Review

_____
_____
_____
_____
_____
_____
_____
_____
_____
_____
_____
_____
_____
_____
_____
_____
_____
_____

REFLECTION
_____
_____
_____

Fabulous Five

Date___/___/___

Today, I am most excited about-

Thankful thoughts:

Learning lessons:

☆ ☆ ☆ — ☆ ☆ ☆

Today I will...

_____
_____
_____
_____
_____
_____
_____
_____
_____
_____
_____
_____

☆ ☆ ☆ — ☆ ☆ ☆

What was the best thing about today? What am I celebrating?

My Daily Review

_____

_____

_____

_____

_____

_____

_____

_____

_____

_____

_____

_____

_____

_____

_____

_____

REFLECTION

_____

_____

_____

Fabulous Five

Date____/____/___

Today, I am most excited about-

★ ☆ ★ — ★ ☆ ★

Today I will...

_____
_____
_____
_____
_____
_____
_____
_____
_____
_____
_____
_____
_____

Thankful thoughts:

Learning lessons:

★ ☆ ★ — ★ ☆ ★

What was the best thing about today? What am I celebrating?

My Daily Review

_____
_____
_____
_____
_____
_____
_____
_____
_____
_____
_____
_____
_____
_____
_____

REFLECTION _____
_____
_____

Fabulous Five

Date___/___/___

Today, I am most excited about-

Thankful thoughts:

Learning lessons:

☆ ☆ ☆ — ☆ ☆ ☆

Today I will...

_____
_____
_____
_____
_____
_____
_____
_____
_____
_____
_____
_____

☆ ☆ ☆ — ☆ ☆ ☆

What was the best thing about today? What am I celebrating?

My Daily Review

REFLECTION

Fabulous Five

Date____/____/____

Today, I am most excited about-

Thankful thoughts:

Learning lessons:

★ ★ ★ — ★ ★ ★

Today I will...

_____

_____

_____

_____

_____

_____

_____

_____

_____

_____

_____

★ ★ ★ — ★ ★ ★

What was the best thing about today? What am I celebrating?

My Daily Review

_____
_____
_____
_____
_____
_____
_____
_____
_____
_____
_____
_____
_____
_____
_____
_____

REFLECTION
_____
_____
_____

Fabulous Five

Date___/___/___

Today, I am most excited about-

★ ☆ ★ — ★ ☆ ★

Today I will...

_____
_____
_____
_____
_____
_____
_____
_____
_____
_____
_____
_____

★ ☆ ★ — ★ ☆ ★

Thankful thoughts:

Learning lessons:

What was the best thing about today? What am I celebrating?

My Daily Review

_____

_____

_____

_____

_____

_____

_____

_____

_____

_____

_____

_____

_____

_____

_____

_____

REFLECTION _____

_____

Fabulous Five

Date____/____/____

Today, I am most excited about-

☆ ☆ ☆ — ☆ ☆ ☆

Today I will...

_____
_____
_____
_____
_____
_____
_____
_____
_____
_____
_____
_____
_____

Thankful thoughts:

Learning lessons:

☆ ☆ ☆ — ☆ ☆ ☆

What was the best thing about today? What am I celebrating?

My Daily Review

_____
_____
_____
_____
_____
_____
_____
_____
_____
_____
_____
_____
_____
_____
_____
_____
_____

REFLECTION _____
_____
_____

Fabulous Five

Date____/____/____

Today, I am most excited about-

Thankful thoughts:

Learning lessons:

Today I will...

_____
_____
_____
_____
_____
_____
_____
_____
_____
_____
_____
_____
_____
_____

What was the best thing about today? What am I celebrating?

My Daily Review

_____
_____
_____
_____
_____
_____
_____
_____
_____
_____
_____
_____
_____
_____
_____
_____

REFLECTION _____
_____
_____
_____

Fabulous Five

Date____/____/____

Today, I am most excited about-

Thankful thoughts:

Learning lessons:

★ ☆ ★ — ★ ☆ ★

Today I will...

_____
_____
_____
_____
_____
_____
_____
_____
_____
_____
_____
_____
_____
_____

★ ☆ ★ — ★ ☆ ★

What was the best thing about today? What am I celebrating?

My Daily Review

REFLECTION

Fabulous Five

Date____/____/____

Today, I am most excited about-

Thankful thoughts:

Learning lessons:

☆ ☆ ☆ — ☆ ☆ ☆

Today I will...

_____
_____
_____
_____
_____
_____
_____
_____
_____
_____
_____
_____

☆ ☆ ☆ — ☆ ☆ ☆

What was the best thing about today? What am I celebrating?

My Daily Review

_____

_____

_____

_____

_____

_____

_____

_____

_____

_____

_____

_____

_____

_____

_____

_____

REFLECTION _____

_____

_____

Fabulous Five

Date____/____/____

Today, I am most excited about-

Thankful thoughts:

Learning lessons:

★ ★ ★ — ★ ★ ★

Today I will...

_____
_____
_____
_____
_____
_____
_____
_____
_____
_____
_____

★ ★ ★ — ★ ★ ★

What was the best thing about today? What am I celebrating?

My Daily Review

_____
_____
_____
_____
_____
_____
_____
_____
_____
_____
_____
_____
_____
_____
_____
_____
_____
_____

REFLECTION

Fabulous Five

Date____/____/____

Today, I am most excited about-

★ ☆ ★ — ★ ☆ ★

Today I will...

_____
_____
_____
_____
_____
_____
_____
_____
_____
_____
_____
_____
_____

★ ☆ ★ — ★ ☆ ★

Thankful thoughts:

Learning lessons:

What was the best thing about today? What am I celebrating?

My Daily Review

_____

_____

_____

_____

_____

_____

_____

_____

_____

_____

_____

_____

_____

_____

_____

_____

REFLECTION _____

_____

_____

Fabulous Five

Date____/____/____

Today, I am most excited about-

Thankful thoughts:

Learning lessons:

★ ★ ★ — ★ ★ ★

Today I will...

_____
_____
_____
_____
_____
_____
_____
_____
_____
_____
_____
_____
_____

★ ★ ★ — ★ ★ ★

What was the best thing about today? What am I celebrating?

My Daily Review

_____
_____
_____
_____
_____
_____
_____
_____
_____
_____
_____
_____
_____
_____
_____
_____
_____
_____

REFLECTION
_____
_____
_____

Fabulous Five

Today, I am most excited about-

☆ ☆ ☆ — ☆ ☆ ☆

Today I will...

_____
_____
_____
_____
_____
_____
_____
_____
_____
_____
_____
_____
_____

Thankful thoughts:

Learning lessons:

☆ ☆ ☆ — ☆ ☆ ☆

What was the best thing about today? What am I celebrating?

148

My Daily Review

_____
_____
_____
_____
_____
_____
_____
_____
_____
_____
_____
_____
_____
_____
_____
_____
_____
_____
_____
_____

REFLECTION

Fabulous Five

Date____/____/____

Today, I am most excited about-

☆ ☆ ☆ — ☆ ☆ ☆

Today I will...

_____
_____
_____
_____
_____
_____
_____
_____
_____
_____
_____
_____
_____
_____

☆ ☆ ☆ — ☆ ☆ ☆

Thankful thoughts:

Learning lessons:

What was the best thing about today? What am I celebrating?

My Daily Review

_____
_____
_____
_____
_____
_____
_____
_____
_____
_____
_____
_____
_____
_____
_____
_____

REFLECTION
_____
_____
_____
_____

Fabulous Five

Date____/____/____

Today, I am most excited about-

★ ☆ ✿ — ✿ ☆ ✿

Today I will...

_____
_____
_____
_____
_____
_____
_____
_____
_____
_____
_____
_____

★ ☆ ✿ — ✿ ☆ ✿

Thankful thoughts:

Learning lessons:

What was the best thing about today? What am I celebrating?

My Daily Review

_____
_____
_____
_____
_____
_____
_____
_____
_____
_____
_____
_____
_____
_____
_____
_____
_____

REFLECTION
_____
_____
_____

Fabulous Five

Date____/____/____

Today, I am most excited about-

Thankful thoughts:

Learning lessons:

☆ ☆ ☆ — ☆ ☆ ☆

Today I will...

_____
_____
_____
_____
_____
_____
_____
_____
_____
_____
_____
_____

☆ ☆ ☆ — ☆ ☆ ☆

What was the best thing about today? What am I celebrating?

My Daily Review

_____
_____
_____
_____
_____
_____
_____
_____
_____
_____
_____
_____
_____
_____
_____
_____
_____

REFLECTION
_____
_____
_____

Fabulous Five

Today, I am most excited about-

Thankful thoughts:

Learning lessons:

★ ★ ★ — ★ ★ ★

Today I will...

_____
_____
_____
_____
_____
_____
_____
_____
_____
_____
_____
_____
_____
_____

★ ★ ★ — ★ ★ ★

What was the best thing about today? What am I celebrating?

My Daily Review

REFLECTION

Printed in the United States
By Bookmasters